The View We're Granted

T0306380

Johns Hopkins: Poetry and Fiction
John T. Irwin, General Editor

The View We're Granted

Poems by Peter Filkins

The Johns Hopkins University Press
Baltimore

This book has been brought to publication with the generous assistance of the Albert Dowling Trust and the Writing Seminars Publication Fund.

© 2012 The Johns Hopkins University Press
All rights reserved. Published 2012
Printed in the United States of America on acid-free paper
9 8 7 6 5 4 3 2 1

The Johns Hopkins University Press
2715 North Charles Street
Baltimore, Maryland 21218-4363
www.press.jhu.edu

Library of Congress Cataloging-in-Publication Data

Filkins, Peter.
The view we're granted / by Peter Filkins.
p. cm. — (Johns Hopkins, poetry and fiction)
ISBN 978-1-4214-0632-9 (pbk. : alk. paper) — ISBN 978-1-4214-0704-3 (electronic) — ISBN 1-4214-0632-2 (pbk. : alk. paper) — ISBN 1-4214-0704-3 (electronic)
I. Title.
PS3556.I4288V54 2012
811'.54—dc23 2011053061

A catalog record for this book is available from the British Library.

Special discounts are available for bulk purchases of this book. For more information, please contact Special Sales at 410-516-6936 or specialsales@press.jhu.edu.

The Johns Hopkins University Press uses environmentally friendly book materials, including recycled text paper that is composed of at least 30 percent post-consumer waste, whenever possible.

To the memory of my sister

Here between the hither and farther shore
While time is withdrawn, consider the future
And the past with an equal mind.

T. S. Eliot, "The Dry Salvages"

And now, with gleams of half-extinguished thought,
With many recognitions dim and faint,
And somewhat of a sad perplexity,
The picture of the mind revives again.

William Wordsworth, "Lines Composed a Few Miles above Tintern Abbey"

Contents

The View We're Granted

I

Dismantling the Birches

for James Lasdun

"Topped, dropped & chipped 2 dead white birch trees"
reads the bill arriving one week later.
The damage? "Labor & Equipment—$250,"
though it's no sure bargain: blithe empty air
now all that's left of what once stood, who knows,
a lifetime? a century? their tall, swaying might
reduced to firewood we'll burn this winter.

Still, it was time. The birches too near the house,
one windy night a heavy limb broke loose,
waking us with a *thunk* so loud we thought
the end of sleep had come, our roof done in
and leaking through November's bony cold
until next morning workers broke the news:
nothing for it, those trees were coming down.

Summer. Morning. A locust's rising whine,
the day a promise caught in each flickering leaf,
as a boy I loved their white thrusting shoots
rising like a massive V outside my window,
each trunk's diameter twice my arm across,
the scarred papery bark a sheet inscribed
with twists and leanings, weather written in.

How many summers had they seen? How many kites
had disemboweled flight among their branches?
And who could know what kind of pure good luck
had let them grow so tall, lightning blasts
and blight, drought and shearing winds, the gamut
of experience as like to strike them down
as nurture lasting reach into a pale blue sky.

I blink my eyes, but yes, they're really gone,
leaving behind an absence that becomes them,
sawdust and firewood cleared away as well,
the view pried open to reveal a landscape,
one never really seen before—that hilltop,
iron gray in autumn, a stillness loud with geese
on their necessary flight above the trees.

The Hunters

for Susan

Dawn's pewter light
erupts with a blast
of shotguns on the lake,
jolting us awake
from our halting sleep.

The hunters are back,
predictable as fall's
scarlet plash
of calendar maples.
Camouflaged, funereal

in their whispered
deathbed watch
behind a makeshift blind,
their fitful *quack-ack-acks*
imitate the call

of a wounded duck
that in fact sounds drunk,
each belching shot
an attempt at validation
that ends in failure.

Sweetheart, the blaze
of morning is upon us
here in our downy bed.
Come closer. Let's kiss.
Whatever's insinuated

by the chuck of water,
far fields of sun-blanched hay,
may it be this
slow tribulation
of lips and arms and breasts

under the snug duvet
you lift like a vaulted wing,
our bodies warm as
rose light firing the hills
of this furious season.

The News at 10

for Malina and Isabel

Twin shadows fall
from the heights you've grown,
being's supple measure
in a world gone wrong

despite your beauty,
so tender, emergent,
explosive in its gift
to implicate each day

that for what we love
is why we're here to live.

9/12

Another lucid evening in September,
the soccer field aglow with tawny light
glinting off steeples against hills of umber
as kids kick a soccer ball, dribble, then strike,

the game nearing its end, the coach commanding
the defense to advance, bum rush the goalie,
a mob of ten-year-olds soon catapulting
upon each other, erupting in revelry

spearheaded by cheering moms, the odd dad
locked in a fist pump, players on the field
scattered in triumph, the whistle blowing dead
the goal, the game, the evening's last-minute yield

of victory's elixir now sending them off
in a roar of engines through the asphalt dusk,
dew neutralizing the field like a sedative,
or a prayer's ellipsis, quiet as a mosque.

Sunflowers

Like a platoon at taps, heads heavy
with autumn, they stand regardless
of the season's cusp, audacious
in their dress, swollen with seed
of a once and future greenery
they neither command nor possess,
someone's harvest love positing this
late panache of yellow vanity

all along the corn rows, wind
rattling the husks, the silos leaning
inland, the barnyard dimpled by dung,
the hayloft bearing patiently its hint
of open summer dwindling to must
sunflowers auger in the early frost.

The Globe

Blue tilted pupil
staring at heaven,
a child's small hand
can set you spinning.

Countries and borders,
like cataracts,
float on your surface
as passing facts

arranged by history,
shifted by wars,
erased by time
like dinosaurs,

while you on your own
are ignorant of pain,
geography's game plan:
simply remain.

But should we vacate
your azure premises,
who will there be
to measure the distances

from ocean to landfall,
from equator to cap;
who will there be
to color the map?

No matter. Don't worry.
It's not your concern.
Another sun sets,
another Troy burns,

as you circumnavigate
the core of your being
—empty dead air,
cardboard and printing.

Owen's Shark

I

When young Harold caught it, reeling it in,
raucous, incredulous laughter soon ceasing
as his father helped him land the shark
and beat its head in, hammering, hammering
until the great gray length of it lay still,

no one could imagine that later, unable
to resist another peek at triumph
before bedtime, he'd find the shark
standing upright on its tail, alive
and menacing as he ran to Wilfred,

begging him come see it, which soon
he did, the boys later convincing their father
to let the fish go, take it back to the bay,
where for weeks they saw it swimming
in the cold swift waters of the Irish Sea.

II

“It is a great life,” Wilfred later wrote,
oblivious to “the ghostly glimmering of guns,
the hollow crashing of the shells,” the front
feeling like “neither France nor England,
but a kind of paddock where the beasts
are kept a few days before the shambles,”

as he was, dying a week before war’s end,
leading his platoon across a muddy canal
they’d captured, then lost, then captured again
without him, who had reminded his mother,
“There is no danger, or if any, it will be
well over before you read these lines.”

III

And so the shark swam, portside
to the *Astraea*, Greek goddess of justice,
launched on the day of Wilfred's birth,
but cruising now off the coast of Africa,
the armistice signed, while Harold was sure

the man who sat in his cabin before him
was indeed Wilfred, silent and smiling,
his eyes "alive with the familiar look
of trying to make me understand,"
though what it was he didn't know

in the warm waters north of Alexandria,
where legend has it that a shark
escorting any ship is thought a sign
of a good day's catch, harbor nets teeming
with the pale, bruised bodies of the dead.

Solitaire

When I saw *The Downfall* in Berlin,
the theater just around the corner
from the long-buried bunker, I couldn't believe
Frau Goebbels would sit down to a game
of solitaire after having just killed
all six of her children as they slept,
cyanide preferable to what she imagined
the Russians would do once they moved in.

Who, indeed, could maintain such composure?
Especially at such a time, lights flickering
out and then on like the Führer's rages,
her children expiring with a last shudder
echoed on screen by the bunker's quaking.

I couldn't accept it. Too ironic
a turn, too convenient a portrayal,
the director telling us this is what started it,
millions of dead and wounded the result
of repression, the will to power, a woman
snapping down cards to the rattle of gunfire.

But what if it was like that, Frau Goebbels
unable to think of anything better to do
amid such ruin, except to wait
for her beloved Reich to finally topple
and release her from her nightmare?

The next day, visiting Sachsenhausen,
I learned about a group of prisoners
who at night had continued practicing
scales and arpeggios, a Dvořák quartet,
secretly in the hold of the pathology lab,
where by day the bodies were dissected
in search of abnormalities, myself
transfixed while I sat there listening
to the audio guide, the prisoners' seeming
need for dignity in the teeth of death
comprised of a courage few of us know.

Or could hope to, trapped as we are
by certain limitations, no one surviving
who witnesses the woman playing solitaire,
the man inside the refurbished museum
thinking about a handful of musicians
practicing a transcription of Schubert's Eighth,
elusive and abandoned, unfinished forever.

Chinatown

That night over dinner when he told me
about the affair that he'd been having
as his wife lay dying, her lungs awash
with cancer, his voice betraying a wave
of guilt that would soon pull him under,

I thought of *Chinatown*, and how
Jack Nicholson can't see the future
as the past coming at him, Faye Dunaway
being no more than the ravishing
vehicle of his own familiar doom.

The evil we do can seem so accidental,
our best intentions somehow misleading us,
and yet John Huston's craggy gentility
is there to remind us how very petty
and self-serving great wrongs often are.

Which explains nothing, of course, nor would
we want it to, just as in the voice
of my friend I heard those ravages
let loose like so much displaced water
scouring down the gorges outside of L.A.,

while in the end Jack Nicholson remains
stunned on a street corner, wanting
only to keep a woman from being hurt,
yet ensuring she was, the sympathy we feel
too easily embraced to be understood.

Requiem for the Body Snatchers

for Lawrence Raab

It's hard to tell when things no longer seemed
the same. "Such peace," I'd say to Becky, "so little
complication. It makes you wonder what
we saw in all that bother." Though who could know
trouble was still with us despite the change.

For it wasn't until the first real death occurred
that I began to worry. Irma Williams, 39,
mother of two and at the peak of health.
I still recall the day she first walked in,
something about the hidden way she smiled
that, oddly enough, recalled the smell of rain,
though I thought nothing of it. *Terminal infestation*
was what I calmly wrote. *Prepare new pod*
to replicate the body, dismissing her
with a note and the usual array of pills
to bring on sleep, just like a thousand others,
now and then a broken bone or complex fracture
seeming worth the effort, while most I knew
were as easily replaced as healed.

Her question, however, should have tipped me off,
how hesitantly she asked it while buttoning her blouse:
What happens to our bodies when they're finished?
I sat her down and quickly explained the process,
how, long ago, out of the sky had come

a solution: intergalactic seeds adrift,
which landed in Roy Abrahm's field and grew
those replicas we thought so unlike us,
yet spelled our true salvation, redeeming all
the cares and worries chronic to these shells
in which we walk around.

                                        Whatever stirred
inside of Irma betrayed her blank-eyed stare
puzzled now with longing, though at the time
I'd no idea just what it was—some kind
of shadow passion, some tic, like a thirst for salt
or hankerings to weep our bodies sometimes get.
But when they found her afloat in Crescent Lake
I knew I'd missed a sign.

                                        "Miles, O Miles,
it doesn't really matter," Becky assured me
that night upon the patio gazing up at stars.
"Everything's still the same. You sleep, you wake,
you eat and go to work, nothing more
than who gets dinner or takes out the trash
to occupy your mind. Irma's dead.
But there's plenty of us around. You're just a doctor,
and it's like you always said: Leave grief
to the specialists, though by now they must be gone."

We're always in the wrong it seems when most
we think our world secure, for I'll admit
when reports came in of strange things happening
—music heard at night, distant hillside fires—

I had my doubts, despite each small alarm:
patients stopping in who'd complain of nerves,
mysterious aches, the odd funereal dream
they couldn't comprehend, but thought an omen,
or a boy who said his father wasn't his father
but one big nasty mood.

Then more bodies were found.
The entire town awash with rumor—damaged
strain of pods, rogue viruses on the loose—
I was a man of science having to face the truth:
something was inside us, something inherent
to whatever code was written in these bodies,
but whose meaning is a cipher, the problem being
there is no difference you can actually see
between yourself and them, the trouble's inside you
and has been all along.

The mind is strange
and wonderful, but hardly knows itself.
Who'd have thought that I could tire of Becky,
envying now her drug-like calm. She'd insist
my moods were hallucinations brought on by stress,
though deep inside my newfound heart I felt
raw as a septic wound. "Relax!" she said.
"It's just a passing phase. They may be dead
and dying, but tell me, where's the odds in that?
Miles, we're built for lasting. Desire, ambition,
malignancies like love, they're nothing but
completely normal mysteries we long ago gave up,
while as for aging, please, I'd rather take a pill."

And yet, plagued by constant low-grade longing,
I felt a failure. Reveries at sunset,
anxieties at noon, even my memory
held me prisoner, reaching back for songs
whose meaning I once knew but had forgotten,
such as *It's summer and the moon is full*
and I know a bank where the wild thyme grows,
unconscious urgings driving me crazy until
late one night I packed a bag, and breathing hard,
stood alone downstairs, my heart lit up with panic,
guilt knocking at its walls. In recent weeks
so much had been discovered, anything was possible.
Spouses suddenly gone, secret late-night trysts,
maybe someone was really out there waiting
to welcome me home, yet who could know for sure?

Up here beside the fire I cannot think
Becky is wrong, but just delayed, a matter of time
before she comprehends such local infestations
permanent as the past—mutant, sad
humanity having returned with a vengeance
born of the pleasures of this waking sleep
habitual with dying. Anger? Self-pity?
It's true, they plague us now, but also compassion
for those desperate creatures, heads tilted skyward,
searching for an answer they've yet to find
was always meant to be denied them,
imperfect as that is, while no doubt for Becky
certain and unavoidable, maddening as a dream.

II

Sirens

Severing the air
of calm they prevail
upon the ear

perpetual
as mantras to gods
invoking collateral

against the odds
in this neighborhood
of pain in pyramids,

something understood.

Vermeer

The Art of Painting, *ca. 1666*

I

The news from Delft is still the same:
plague has returned, the ships have left,
while farther north the sea at Haarlem
is flat and gray, cold as the deft
chill lens that amplifies this room
unto itself, history being elsewhere
and unknowable. Though Clio may consume
provinces, countries, her golden hair
is wrapped in laurel, securely intact,
while what remains is what is seen
in deep perspective, the painted fact
of light that dwells, this dwelling scene.

II

Another child is dead and buried,
the cold clods raining upon his casket
no longer heard, lost to the harried
wastes of time where an angel's trumpet
lifts its muted anthem toward infinity.
Still the music plays, each note
expressed through an anonymity
treasured by lovers, lining the rote
familiar charm of each everyday task
stretched on a canvas's snowy expanse,
as the moment congeals, alive in a mask
whose life is an art attuned to silence.

III

The map of things is enigmatic:
a room, a girl, a trumpet's sheen.
Yet what peels back the curtain's fabric
enlivens what the mind has seen.
Her limp blond curls, demure blue dress
pooling color like a low-lit flame,
are but the holy surfaces
of life embroidered by a frame.
Beyond this, nothing. Rumors, death,
the sky a leaden plate above.
By canvas skin, by brush's breath,
master, you no doubt were loved.

Rocky

As the fastball released, spinning and spinning
to slide invincibly low and away, how could
I know (the umpire calling me out, out
went the roar of the crowd into the dusky air)
that years later, blear-eyed mad, he'd place

the gun in his mouth, maybe think twice
about the mess he'd leave behind, certainty
however triumphing over the future
blank empty of her touch, her smile
no more now than heartsick scorching flame

triggering the radical inner explosion
of a life gone to pieces, Rocky! Rocky!
his father bellowed from the backdoor steps
as we played on and on in the sandlot,
practicing the useless beautiful skills

of our Little League, pop fly and grounder,
toss and catch, there in the low red glare
of a late inning's summer sunset that,
come Saturday, would freeze my stance,
blind me to the pitch, I never saw it coming.

Girl, 2, Pulled from Pond

Was it the light
  that caught you,
recondite
  as angel breath,
was it the light
  that drew you
in your summer dress?

Was it the song
  of a blackbird
con-quer-ińg
  with its call,
was it the song
  of a blackbird,
and that was all?

Was it the scent
  of sweet clover
that, dizzying, sent
  you into the field,
was it the scent
  of sweet clover,
that so appealed?

Was it the cool
  feel of water,
the pond's muddy ooze
  sucking each toe,
was it the cool
  feel of water
that tempted you so?

A jitterbug shadow
  with wide-open arms
crossing the meadow
  that parted like air;
soon everywhere howls
  sown by alarm
and you not there.

Beanbag Toss

About the size of a book.
Homemade. Filled with
a pound of navy beans
sewn into corduroy swatches
of your worn-out, crimson
best-for-playground jeans.

All morning we'd watch
cartoons while tossing
its nubbed, gravelly weight
between us on the rug,
dust kicking up in motes
aswirl with each new chuck

across the cellar playroom,
the comfort of its heft
exiting my hand to sail,
in memory, the length
of air emptied as
you caught it, then left.

Marking Time

Denise Evelyn Filkins, 1959–2001

Five years have passed, no, six since that early spring
when, having heard you'd died, I stood alone beneath
a full moon drifting through a cloudless sky beyond
your leaving, its hard mercurial sheen now falling
on the dewy fields, now glimmering yet
upon the lake, augmented by the dark
secluded shadows inked below its passing.

And still you're gone. The moment, like all others,
sportive in its little hermit's game of hide-
and-seek, as at my desk a line familiar as
"The day is come when I again repose"
can set me remembering that you went to bed
thinking you'd wake up, but didn't, or maybe did
and found yourself tossing in that murky black
where the fretful stir unprofitable. Sis,
whatever fear or worry strained your sickened heart
was soon no more, voided as it was by you
putting up a sign announcing CLOSED FOR GOOD,
while ever since for me that "still, sad music"
is just that—still sad, if not harsh and grating.

Yet you are with me here, with me here again,
where neither that moon nor you exist, but live
tethered to this memory composed of words
aimed hopelessly at transcribing what once was

our "all in all," now half of it gone, nothing but to try,
remembering as I do that childhood spent
completing the circuit of this dead-end road
where I still live, our whirring, rattly bikes
flying the gravel of the lakeside drive,
while later on, beneath a sickle moon,
games of blindman's buff or kick the can
played with the other kids would find us thrilled
as fugitives in the night that was and is
felt in the blood and felt along the heart
and is no more, is unremembered pleasure.

Still, marking time in dribs and drabs, I sit
wintering through among these many shapes
and lines and recognitions dim and faint
as outside snow falls benignly down and down,
burying the roads, blanketing the fields,
the farms, the lake, the lonely houseless woods
one should shy away from to seek someone to love,
though I push on, the better part of each day
spent chasing what cannot be caught: time's sift-
ing, shapeless give-and-take that takes and takes
amid the squall defining and the wind that shapes
these contours in the snow.

Just why, who knows?
To evoke your spirit? Tall orders soon are failed,
though oddly, missing you conjures up a voice
that, while counter, fits these scribblings. Sis, if you
are there, forgive these tainted measures, powerless
as they are to erase whatever fear or pain

or grief was yours, and which I hope was freed
within your passing. Meanwhile, I'm still here,
living near that hill where we once played as kids,
rolling and rolling until we bottomed out,
arms folded on our chests, each of us breathless
with those squeals of laughter continuing to spill
down through all the years of this our life
and its unmaking, on which I've dwelled here
to pass the time with you while trying to hold
both you and it in place, and having done so,
if not for yours, at least for someone's sake.

III

Speed Skaters

Stroke and glide, crossover
and arch, speed skaters lean
into the teeth of winter,

powering through, serene
as the curves they race,
gravity contravened

on a sun-glazed surface
configured as oval,
blades gripping the ice—

breathlessly formal.

The View

Arranging it would be half the fun
  if it weren't for the bother.
Mountains set in place, receding hues
  of purplish green gone yellow,
then reddish brown, could act as backdrop
  to our private valley, as above,
let loose on throngs of air, a hawk
  circles the empire of a field.

And yet the view we're granted is
  just that: arbitrary but fixed,
whole lifetimes spent staring at a square
  of boxed-in scenery we call
a window, outside of which may be
  a pond in autumn, a maple
dropping its leaves, or the spectacular
  ambulation of a noonday wren.

Alley or backyard, seascape or porch,
  what's seen remains our measure
of those day-lit declinations
  traversing the brickwork, busying
the harbor with platinum glitter,
  or in muted, snowbound winter
imbuing the pine tree with a chill
  luminescence empty of wind.

What use then the leveraged desire
  for those commanding vistas
propped on hillsides consuming the glen?
  None is more refined
than an afternoon's march of shadows
  printing the lawn with fence posts,
as one looks on, appreciating
  the stony gravitas of yard,

where the constant flittings of the wren
  here outside my window
are amplitude enough as twilight
  infiltrates the study curtains
left open to gather in the view
  that, closing down, ignites
those soft penumbras articulating
  the fence posts, the wren, the grass.

Waterfall, Rock, Trout

for Richard Wilbur

I

Half a mile upstream, culled by an eddy,
subsurface sinewy swirls set in motion
the river's emerging character, boulders bend-
ing currents upon each other, releasing energy
whose coursing pulse becomes a colloquy
of runnels and rivulets, rills and fens
soon gathering force, their forward propulsion
mounted by the pull of phantom gravity

swift now through a narrow throaty run
that whips the water white as ivory,
clotting in whirlpools lustrous with sun,
as the river bottoms out, at last set free
to race the gully's granite walls until
it hits those weathered falls and spills and spills.

II

Stasis in flux, a massy knob of granite
planted downstream by a long lost eon
of Mesozoic drift—polished, worn down
by scything currents, yet no less adamant
or real, the mute immediate lug of it
unfazed by the river's press and drone,
its frozen magma a squat imperial throne,
the once and future king of the spinning planet.

III

Clever as sunlight padding a forest floor,
trout appear and disappear, torpedo shapes
patrolling under the shoreline's catkin lips.
Furtive, shy—dissembling is their nature,
the darting trick of it an inner spur
to subterranean litheness giving the slip
to fly or hook, intelligence in the grip
of fins on currents of the iced-down water.

Call it a blessing, call it a lucky strike
to watch their wary calm beneath the falls,
heads pointed upstream, tails gently aquiver,
the sun at certain angles able to make
their speckled bodies glow as if immutable,
suspended in the flow of the flowing river.

A Certain Grammar

My neighbor re-caning a summer chaise,
seventy-eight and patiently unrolling
green and yellow lengths that stretch
with little dips and rises crossing,
weaving beneath him a simple pattern
amid the motion of his blurring hands
next to the lake's cool glacial water.

Until he's lost, perhaps, in thought
while trying to remember the time
he first decided to keep repairing
the chair, the docks, the rotting boat,
rather than buy or build them anew,
refusing, at least, a part of his life
to change—its passive tense, its verb.

Weatherwise

To know the sleet
   in the heart of the squall,
its flat-liner pelt
   of incoming tracers,

is also to know
   the path of the storm
grinding the seabed,
   lashing the breakwater

before turning inland
   to the taciturn
provinces, the low
   frontal pressure

shaping these pellets
   ticking the windshield,
the gleaming blacktop,
   the long ride home.

A Country Quilt

I

It meant something, of course, back in a time
when winter asked a patience that demanded
the algebra of pattern beneath an oily lamp
to steady the mind through provinces of gray
relentless boredom on the point of a pin.

Calico and chintz, prints and palampores,
mordants and madders locked up in their dyes,
an evening spent stitching blocks of color
was one less wasted in the lanterned dark

surrounded by wind, snowdrifts rippling
the rocky fields under stars as white
as cotton tufting against the indigo black
of a dream of wandering *Delectable Mountains*,
their gardens and orchards, vineyards and peace.

II

Shiloh, Shenandoah, Antietam, Bull Run—
Grays and Blues soon threaded by history,
trenches, like cording, wound through a landscape
knotted by bodies fixed permanently in crimsons.

Elsewhere *Housetop* turned into *Hog Pen Pole*,
points of needles pricking their owner's conscience,
though still the news came: Mechanicville, Malvern
stippling cerulean with thick cannon smoke.
Six hundred thousand eventually would fall,

never to return to *Pine Tree* or *Thistle*
laid out on four posters offering their balm
of batting and broderie billowing like mercy
upon those who survived the long march home.

III

No calico? Then denim. No muslin? A flour sack.
The stitching as wavy as the creek at Gee's Bend,
Bricklayer, Monkey Wrench, Double Wedding Ring
—syncopated movements of color and time
worn thin as a thought bent over spun flax.

Chance became choice, the call and response
of Pettways and Mosleys, Bendolphs and Bennetts
creating an art as practical as its pretense
of dignity spawned from a bunch of cloth scraps,

which later, and likely, settled on hunger
in beds packed with bodies four and five deep,
the newspapered walls proffering their headlines:
"Markets Collapse—Failed Banks Overrun,"
as needles go on diving through worn-out sheets.

IV

Naught is naught, figure is figure,
the New Deal looking much like the Old,
although a war will alter it, battalions
sweating in holds plying the Atlantic.

Normandy, Cherbourg, Cologne, and Berlin
sprinkled through letters like silk exotics
in Boston and Birmingham, Memphis or Merrimac,
the hours bleeding together their fugitive tints
for eyes tired of scanning patchwork horizons

while waiting for men to return and draw comfort
in front of televisions soon flickering their blue
sad corteges etching memories like caustic:
the coffin in Atlanta hauled by Gee's Bend mules.

V

The museum is closing. The exhibition finished.
Soon corduroys and cottons will be folded and vanish
into vaults preserving them like sanitized tombs,
the wear of thin fingers, the residue of sweat
sealed off like portfolios in human detritus.

Yet all rows lead to home, somewhere patience
still pleating its worn-out denim or damask,
the staid Palladian charm of the Boston MFA
hardly a match for each spread that fashions

its alchemy of time and deft labor, salvage
the catalyst for each reticulated equation
of fabric, of color, of pure grim necessity
balanced by pride and a pronounced humility
radiant as *Sunburst*, indelible as *Stars*.

Letter to Susan in Seattle

I

Your letter, six months dormant on my shelf,
appears mid-morning among the books and dust,
aspirin, post cards, pens, a broken cup,
and asks me how I am. Answer? Well.
Or is it *was*? This far on it's hard to tell.

Still, details. My winter's gone, your autumn
is on its way. Outside, blustery March wind
showers New York with trash, while I imagine
September stirs the salmon to their final run
into the bay. What I've passed, you've begun

six months ago, three thousand miles away,
and nothing for it but sit down, pick up a pen,
rummage that bulging file—*What Might Have Been*—
(I imagine you there. I imagine your eyes.)
to offer at least this poem's late reprise

jetting across these fifty United States,
where, this morning, I sit alone in one,
you in another, both of us knowing
our separate lives and loves in separate ways,
the private turn of the heart that is a day . . .

II

Or three decades? This morning, two rooms away
I hear you stir in bed, namesake of someone other.
The house, the kids asleep, our life together
breathe all around me as I find myself
staring at expired goods on an unmarked shelf:

the poem left unfinished, a friendship lost,
thirty years gone by, happenstance and age
abandoning as well what was written on the page
—or might have been, or even you'd approve
as heedless art revised by present love.

Forgive me, Susan, it's difficult to write
and live each day remaining as we do
caught in the web of those we loved and knew,
six months, three decades later, memory's refrain
confabulating the past, reminding me again

life's revealed in glimpses: that winning wave
you flash within a crowd so able to impart
those tender intimations of the heart
felt in autumn, old letters, a salmon's brilliant bow . . .
The lives we come to write are the lives we know.

Constable's Clouds

for Fred H. Stocking

I

Scudding through distances, hovering in blue
vacuities of a summer's day, cumuli
float upon the surface of a ranging eye
that studies their shape, analyzes their hue

in pigments now aswirl upon the palette,
soft collisions of white and spectral gray
soon weathering the canvas, capturing a day
whose transience we know because he saw it

there in the changeable sky he stood beneath,
stratus and nimbus, thunderhead and puff
fixed in their currency, the consequence of
the raw prevailing wind on Hampstead Heath.

II

"No two days are alike, nor even two hours,"
and so his brush keeps on the move while he
does not, despising those who continually
ignore their craft by "running after pictures."

Weymouth, Harrow, Flatford, Dedham Vale,
ephemera beneath the sky's broad radius
casting England's neutral light on all that is
and eludes him, be it fame, or more so the pale

"evening light off a dark grey effect—looking
eastwards" toward a drifting bank of cloud
that's there, then gone, someone in the crowd
later calling his picture "a nasty green thing."

III

Maria coughs again, the taste of blood
causing a cloud of fear to pass across
her feverish bright-eyed gaze. Soon loss
will fell him. "Every gleam of sunshine blighted,

can it be wondered I paint continual storms?"
Each gathering front, each rising eastern gale
turbid now with grief, as wind and hail
consume a placid landscape, unleashing forms

that build and threaten, yet do not release
him from the sadness planted in his heart,
the demands of composition, the rigor of art
as equal to rain as sun, adversity as peace.

IV

“I shall never feel again as I have felt,
the face of the world is totally changed to me.”
And yet the sketches continue, originality
hard won upon the back of a life that’s dealt

with sorrow by studying atmospheric effects.
“Clouds. Moving very fast. With occasional
very bright openings to the blue,” the residual
of an altocumulus inhabiting the flex

of a brushstroke, “wind after rain in morning”
the note he jots to catalogue the weather
he’ll use, if not survive, observing much later,
“in truth, my art is another word for feeling.”

The Broken Piano

Have all your melodies left you,
  your keyboard idle as dentures,
voided now of its raggedy tunes?

Even so, time still plays you,
  abandoned in this drafty barn,
where at night the mouse's struggle

ekes out its panicked syncopation
  beneath the owl's wheeling shadow
as a shutter clatters in the manic wind.

Winter having chilled you, summer
  expanding your soundboard's grain,
music, like desolation, has become

for you an opus cordoned off
  by shrieks and groans, broken strings
whose memory of a hammer's blow

is sweetened by a finger's touch
  somewhere coaxing out a last scherzo
before dissonant, cold neglect set in.

And yet you remain, upright, serene,
  your impassive bulk anchoring the dark
hushed rafters, the hayloft poised to hear

the concert of your ruin, silence
  the answering choir whose crescendo
is final and certain, harrowing the applause.

A Stand of Maple

Either side of the pot-holed postal road
they rise, imperious in their haggard bark
against a stone wall spilling boulders like coins
among caramel-colored rays of winter sun
conceding snowdrift shadow its ice-bound blue.

Soon sap will fill them, swelling sagging veins
of plastic tubing stretched like life support
above mercurial rivulets of melting snow,
while nearby and palpable, hints of green
will rouse a meadow to swaying life again.

And yet for now, frozen in this aching cold,
recalcitrant as a riddle, branches whistling
in a razor wind, who could possibly know
their future a season hibernating in starches
released by fire boiling their sugars clean?

How intrepid and insensible, how unlikely
the world can seem, an empty length of road
boring through maples, bitter capillaries of cold
promising sweetness, irrecusable the thrum
of buckets in springtime, amber on the tongue.

Notes on the Poems

"Owen's Shark": Details and quotes in the poem are from Jon Stallworthy's biography, *Wilfred Owen* (Oxford: Oxford UP, 1974).

"Requiem for the Body Snatchers": The poem is intended as a sequel to the 1956 classic film *Invasion of the Body Snatchers,* directed by Don Siegel. In the film, Dr. Miles Bennell tries to escape the alien pods that reproduce human beings and possess their hosts when they fall asleep. The poem assumes that both Miles and his girlfriend, Becky Driscoll, eventually succumb, but the aliens discover that their bodies prove human and mortal after all. A number of phrases are taken from Daniel Mainwaring's screenplay. The line "It's summer and the moon is full, and I know a bank where the wild thyme grows" is indeed spoken by Miles in the movie and is from *A Midsummer Night's Dream.*

"A Country Quilt": Phrases and information on quilts are from Roderick Kiracofe's catalogue *The American Quilt* (New York: Potter, 1993). Other historical information is from *Gee's Bend: The Women and Their Quilts* (Atlanta: Tinwood Books, 2002).

"Constable's Clouds:" After his marriage to Maria Bicknell in 1816, John Constable (1776–1837) spent several summers making a series of quick oil studies of clouds in the sky over Suffolk on the back of which he would often record the date, time of day, and the weather conditions. Intended as sketches to help him with the clouds and skies of his larger works, these have since become valued by art historians as important influences on the work of Delacroix and the Impressionists. The quotes cited in the poem are either from Constable's own comments on the back of the sketches or from his lectures on painting.

Acknowledgments

My thanks to the editors of the following periodicals in which the poems listed have been published, some of them in slightly different form:

American Arts Quarterly	"Constable's Clouds"
The Hopkins Review	"Girl, 2, Pulled from Pond"
The Iowa Review	"Owen's Shark"
	"Rocky"
	"Waterfall, Rock, Trout"
Pivot	"The Globe"
Salamander	"Beanbag Toss"
Sewanee Review	"The Broken Piano"
Southwest Review	"Vermeer"

Several of the poems also appeared in *Augustine's Vision*, winner of the 2009 New American Press Chapbook Award. "The Hunters" and "Dismantling the Birches" can be found on the website http://www.lyrikline.org in English and in German translation. "Vermeer" received the 2007 Elizabeth Matchett Stover Memorial Award from *Southwest Review*. I also wish to thank the MacDowell Colony for a residency that provided valuable time to generate many of these poems, Bard College at Simon's Rock for a sabbatical leave, and the American Academy in Berlin for a Berlin Prize Fellowship. Special thanks as well to Lawrence Raab, Rosanna Warren, and Vijay Seshadri for their invaluable comments and suggestions along the way.

About the Author

Peter Filkins is the author of two previous books of poems, *What She Knew* (1998) and *After Homer* (2002), as well as the chapbook *Augustine's Vision* (2010). The recipient of a Berlin Prize Fellowship from the American Academy in Berlin, he also has been awarded the Stover Prize in Poetry from *Southwest Review,* the New American Press Chapbook Award, and fellowships from the James Merrill House, MacDowell Colony, Massachusetts Cultural Council, Millay Colony for the Arts, and Yaddo. His poems and translations have appeared in numerous publications, including the *American Poetry Review,* the *American Scholar,* the *Iowa Review,* the *New Republic,* the *Paris Review, Partisan Review, Poetry, Sewanee Review,* and *Southwest Review.* He teaches writing and literature at Bard College at Simon's Rock.

Poetry Titles in the Series

John Hollander, *Blue Wine and Other Poems*
Robert Pack, *Waking to My Name: New and Selected Poems*
Philip Dacey, *The Boy under the Bed*
Wyatt Prunty, *The Times Between*
Barry Spacks, *Spacks Street, New and Selected Poems*
Gibbons Ruark, *Keeping Company*
David St. John, *Hush*
Wyatt Prunty, *What Women Know, What Men Believe*
Adrien Stoutenberg, *Land of Superior Mirages: New and Selected Poems*
John Hollander, *In Time and Place*
Charles Martin, *Steal the Bacon*
John Bricuth, *The Heisenberg Variations*
Tom Disch, *Yes, Let's: New and Selected Poems*
Wyatt Prunty, *Balance as Belief*
Tom Disch, *Dark Verses and Light*
Thomas Carper, *Fiddle Lane*
Emily Grosholz, *Eden*
X. J. Kennedy, *Dark Horses: New Poems*
Wyatt Prunty, *The Run of the House*
Robert Phillips, *Breakdown Lane*
Vicki Hearne, *The Parts of Light*
Timothy Steele, *The Color Wheel*
Josephine Jacobsen, *In the Crevice of Time: New and Collected Poems*
Thomas Carper, *From Nature*
John Burt, *Work without Hope: Poetry by John Burt*
Charles Martin, *What the Darkness Proposes: Poems*
Wyatt Prunty, *Since the Noon Mail Stopped*
William Jay Smith, *The World below the Window: Poems 1937–1997*
Wyatt Prunty, *Unarmed and Dangerous: New and Selected Poems*
Robert Phillips, *Spinach Days*
X. J. Kennedy, *The Lords of Misrule: Poems 1992–2001*
John T. Irwin, ed., *Words Brushed by Music: Twenty-Five Years of the Johns Hopkins Poetry Series*
John Bricuth, *As Long As It's Big: A Narrative Poem*
Robert Phillips, *Circumstances Beyond Our Control: Poems*
Daniel Anderson, *Drunk in Sunlight*
X. J. Kennedy, *In a Prominent Bar in Secaucus: New and Selected Poems, 1955–2007*
William Jay Smith, *Words by the Water*
Wyatt Prunty, *The Lover's Guide to Trapping*
Charles Martin, *Signs & Wonders*
Peter Filkins, *The View We're Granted*